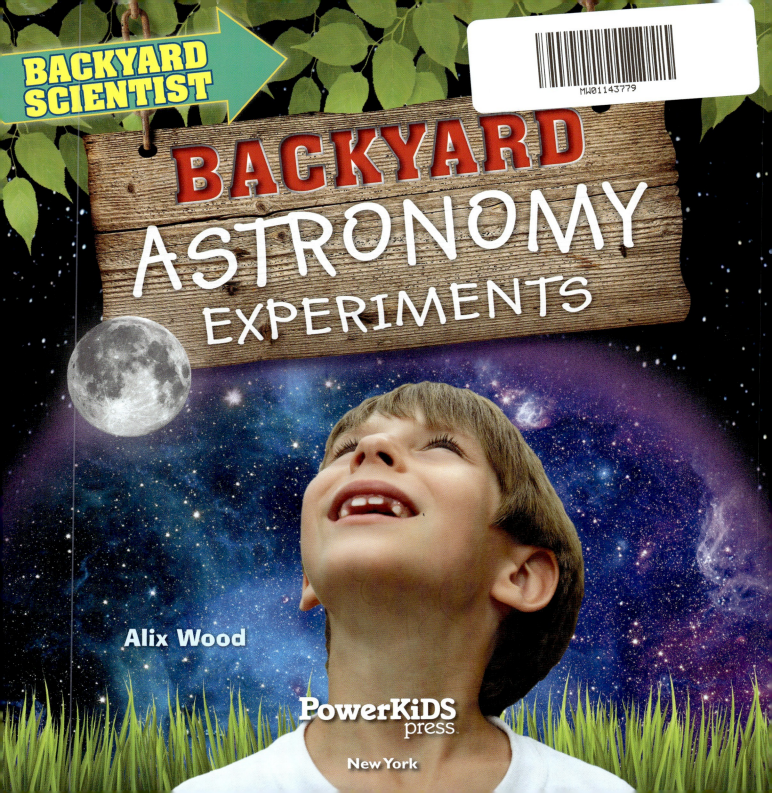

BACKYARD
SCIENTIST

BACKYARD ASTRONOMY EXPERIMENTS

Alix Wood

PowerKiDS press

New York

Published in 2019 by Rosen Publishing
29 East 21st Street, New York, NY 10010

Produced for Rosen Publishing by Alix Wood Books
Designed by Alix Wood
Editor: Eloise Macgregor
Projects devised and photographed by Kevin Wood

Photo credits:
Cover, 1, 4 bottom, 5, 6, 7 left, 13 bottom, 15 left, 16 © Adobe Stock Images;
4 top © Crew of STS-125/NASA; 7 right © mouser; 11 bottom © Takeshi Kuboki;
26 © Shutterstock; all other photos © Kevin Wood

Cataloging-in-Publication Data
Names: Wood, Alix.
Title: Backyard astronomy experiments / Alix Wood.
Description: New York : PowerKids Press, 2019. | Series: Backyard scientist | Includes glossary
and index.
Identifiers: LCCN ISBN 9781538337264 (pbk.) | ISBN 9781538337257 (library bound) |
ISBN 9781538337271 (6 pack)
Subjects: LCSH: Astronomy--Experiments--Juvenile literature.
Classification: LCC QB46.W64 2019 | DDC 520.078--dc2

Printed in the United States of America

CPSIA compliance information: Batch # CS18PK: For Further Information contact Rosen Publishing, New York, New York at 1-800-237-9932.

Contents

What Is Astronomy?

Astronomy is the study of space, and objects in space, such as stars, **comets**, planets, and **galaxies**. For thousands of years people have looked up at the sky, and tried to understand what they saw. People who study astronomy are called astronomers. Astronomers are making important new discoveries as new technology such as space telescopes (right) and powerful rockets help them explore space. It is an exciting time to be an astronomer.

Wonder at the Night Sky

On a clear night, go outside and look up. You don't need a telescope to be amazed by the night sky. The things you can see using just your eyes are incredible. You might see a comet, or a planet, or the International Space Station pass by! Light takes time to travel from space. It takes such a long time that the stars you see may no longer exist!

Setting Up Your Backyard Laboratory

Find an outside space where you can safely do these experiments. Remember to check with whomever owns the space that it is OK to do your experiments there. When you are stargazing, it helps to find a place without too many house and street lights around.

You should be able to find most of the things you will need around your home or yard. You may need to buy some small items, so check the "You Will Need" section before you start a project.

BE SCIENTIFIC

Make notes. Understanding the universe is a little like a huge puzzle. No single astronomer is going to unlock all its secrets by themselves.

Astronomers must make notes about what they discover, and be able to explain their findings to other astronomers. By working together, the puzzles of the universe are much more likely to be solved.

STAYING SAFE

Science experiments can be dangerous. Some of these experiments need you to be outside after dark. Ask a trusted adult to come with you. Take a flashlight and keep yourself safe. During daytime, never look directly at the Sun. It may damage your eyes.

Find a Constellation

A **constellation** is a group of visible stars that form a pattern when seen from Earth. Not all constellations are visible everywhere on Earth, but the constellation Orion can be seen throughout the world. Orion is named after a hunter from a Greek story.

1 Ask an adult to come with you. Go outside on a clear night when there is little or no Moon. Find a spot away from any lights. Let your eyes adjust to the darkness.

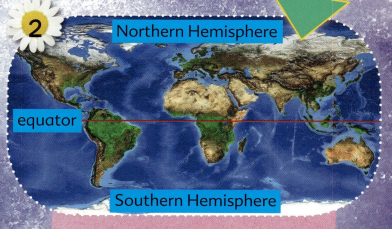

Northern Hemisphere

equator

Southern Hemisphere

2 If you live above the **equator** you are in the northern hemisphere. To find Orion, look in the southwest sky. If you are below the equator, in the southern hemisphere, look in the northwestern sky.

The first thing about Orion that you can usually spot are the three stars known as Orion's belt. Can you find them?

WHAT'S HAPPENING?

Below Orion's belt, three stars make up Orion's sword. The middle star isn't really a star—it's the Orion **nebula**! A nebula is a massive cloud of dust, gas, and **plasma**. They are also often a place where stars are born. The Orion nebula is a big star nursery!

Toilet Roll Solar System

The **solar system** is made up of all the planets, moons, comets, **asteroids**, minor planets, and dust and gas that orbit our Sun. The solar system is vast. Earth's closest neighbor is Venus, which is 25.5 million miles (41 million km) away! Try building a scale model of our solar system.

1

Cut out circles from colored paper to represent each planet and the Sun. Cut out a wiggly shape to be the asteroid belt. Decorate your cutouts using markers, and write their name on them.

2

Place your toilet paper roll on the ground. Place your Sun on the end. Roll out one sheet and tape your Mercury planet cutout onto that sheet. Mercury is the closest planet to the Sun.

3

Continue adding your cutouts to the roll, using the table below. The table tells you how many toilet roll sheets each planet is from the Sun, and the real distance in miles and kilometers.

	Sheets	miles (million)	km (million)
Sun			
Mercury	1	36	58
Venus	2	67	108
Earth	3	93	150
Mars	4	142	228
Asteroid Belt	8	258	416
Jupiter	16	483	778
Saturn	32	887	1,427
Uranus	64	1,783	2,870
Neptune	96	2,794	4,497
Pluto	128	3,635	5,850

4

Do you see why you needed a large space? In this picture, we're not even a quarter of the way through our solar system!

WHAT'S HAPPENING?

The distances in this project are correct, but the planets themselves aren't to scale. The Sun is so large that around 1,300,000 planet Earths could fit inside it! It is its large mass that pulls the planets into **orbit** around it.

Pinhole Sun Gazing

It is very dangerous to look directly at the Sun, but there is a way of viewing the Sun without damaging your eyes. A pinhole viewer safely projects an image of the Sun onto paper. You can use the viewer to look for **sunspots** — darker, cooler areas that appear on the surface of the Sun.

YOU WILL NEED:

- sheet of card stock
- sheet of white paper
- aluminum foil
- a pin
- tape
- scissors
- ruler

ADULT HELP NEEDED

1 Ask an adult to help you cut a square about ³/₄ inch x ³/₄ inch (2 cm x 2 cm) in the center of the card stock. It helps if you push the scissors through the middle of the square first.

2 Place a slightly larger square of aluminum foil over your square hole. Tape it around the edges.

3

Turn the card over. Using a pin, poke a small hole in the center of the foil.

4

On a sunny day, hold the pinhole viewer up so the Sun shines through the hole. Line up the white sheet of paper behind the pinhole viewer. Move the sheet around until you can see an image of the Sun.

WHAT'S HAPPENING?

What you see on your white paper isn't just sunlight shining through the hole, but an actual image of the Sun! Next time a **solar eclipse** takes place, safely watch it using your pinhole viewer. A solar eclipse (right) is when the Moon travels in front of the Sun and blocks its light.

Make an Astrolabe

An astrolabe is a device used by astronomers for measuring the height of objects in the sky. It measures how high above the **horizon** the object is, in degrees (°).

1

Photocopy or trace this template onto paper. Glue the paper to some card stock.

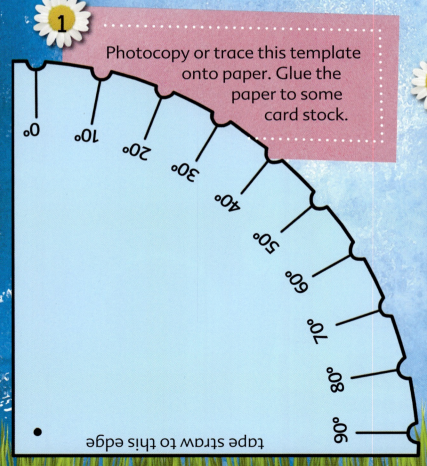

0°
10°
20°
30°
40°
50°
60°
70°
80°
90°

tape straw to this edge

2

Carefully cut around the astrolabe using scissors.

3

Tape the straw along the marked edge of the astrolabe. The straw should not overlap the astrolabe but be taped to the very edge. Trim the straw to fit.

4

Make a hole in the dot near the straw. Thread a length of string slightly longer than one side through the hole. Secure it on the back with tape. Tie the small weight to the end of the string.

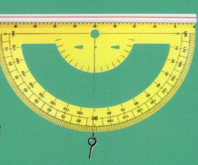

See how to use your astrolabe on page 14.

WHAT'S HAPPENING?

The astrolabe has degrees marked along the rounded edge, just like a protractor. You could make an astrolabe using a protractor, too.

Using Your Astrolabe

Never look at the Sun through your astrolabe, as it will damage your eyes. Track the journey of the Moon through the day, instead. As the Moon travels around Earth, it appears to rise and set just as the Sun does. Measure the different heights that the Moon reaches using your astrolabe.

YOU WILL NEED:

- your astrolabe
- a daytime Moon
- a friend to help you
- a notebook and pen

1 Sit on the ground. Hold the astrolabe so that the curved part is closest to you. Look at the Moon through the straw.

2 Ask a friend to write down the number that lines up with the weighted string. In this photo the reading is 10°. That is how many degrees above the horizon the Moon is.

3

Repeat steps 1 and 2 every half hour and take new readings. Has the Moon changed its height in the sky?

4

There is a way to record the height of the Sun without looking at it. Hold one palm flat. Line up the astrolabe so the Sun shines down the straw and onto your palm. Take a reading. Now you can track the Sun, too.

WHAT'S HAPPENING?

Astrolabes can tell you the height of distant objects. Try it. Walk away from a tree until the astrolabe gives a 45° measurement when you look at the treetop. Measure the height of the astrolabe above the ground, and the distance to the base of the tree. The height of the tree will equal the height of the astrolabe above the ground plus the distance to its base!

The Changing Moon

Have you noticed the Moon appears to change its shape? Go and look at the Moon. What shape is it? Draw 30 circles on paper, and note the shape of the Moon in a circle each day for a month by shading in the dark area. Then try this experiment to learn why we see the different **phases** of the Moon.

May 1st

YOU WILL NEED:

- styrofoam ball
- a long, sharp pencil
- a flashlight
- a pen and paper

ADULT HELP NEEDED

1 Poke the sharp end of a pencil into the styrofoam ball. This ball on a stick will represent the Moon in your experiment.

2 Hold the ball as shown. Ask an adult to point the flashlight toward your Moon. The flashlight is the Sun, and your head is Earth. In this position, your moon will be in shadow, like the picture in the inset blue box.

3

With the flashlight staying still, turn your whole body and arm counterclockwise about 45 degrees. Your Moon is starting to orbit Earth. You should see the right-hand edge of your Moon lit up in a crescent shape.

4

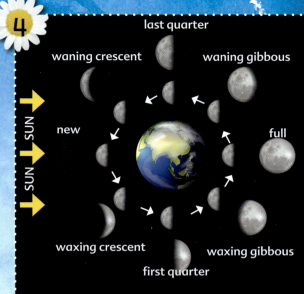

last quarter

waning crescent   waning gibbous

SUN SUN SUN

new

full

waxing crescent   waxing gibbous

first quarter

Keep turning 45 degrees at a time. The outer circle of this diagram shows the phases of the Moon as seen from Earth. The inner circle shows how the Sun lights the Moon during its orbit.

WHAT'S HAPPENING?

The Moon has no light of its own. Moonlight is sunlight bouncing off the Moon's surface. As the Moon orbits Earth, the Sun lights up the side of the Moon that is facing it. To the Sun, it's always a full Moon! Can you predict what shape the Moon will be next week?

Make Your Own Rocket

Gravity in our atmosphere pulls objects toward Earth. To escape Earth's gravity and explore space, astronauts have to use powerful rockets. A rocket is powered when gases shoot out of the back of the rocket at great force. See how this works by building your own simple rocket.

YOU WILL NEED:

- big ball of string
- a straw
- tape
- scissors
- a balloon
- measuring tape
- pen and paper

ADULT HELP NEEDED

1

Thread one end of the string through the straw. You can use gravity to help you do this — hold the straw upright and drop in the string.

2

Tie one end of the string to something stable, such as a garden chair. Holding the other end, step away as far as the string allows you.

3

Ask an adult to blow up a balloon and hold the end without tying it. Then ask them to slide the straw toward you and attach the balloon to the straw using the tape.

4

Release the air from the balloon. You can measure and record how far it travels. Try again holding the string at a different angle.

WHAT'S HAPPENING?

Scientist Isaac Newton discovered that for every action there is an equal and opposite reaction. Your balloon is powered by Newton's law of motion. The force of the air rushing out of your balloon pushes the balloon in the opposite direction. Rockets work in exactly the same way.

Make a Sundial

For centuries before clocks were invented, people used the Sun to tell the time. The Earth revolves around the Sun at a constant speed. Because of this, you can use the Sun to tell you what time it is. A sundial uses the Sun's shadow to point at the right time of day. Try making one and test if it works.

YOU WILL NEED:

- scissors
- transparent tape
- card stock
- a long sharp pencil or skewer
- paper to trace with

ADULT HELP NEEDED

1 Carefully trace this template onto paper. If you can, you could scan or photocopy it instead. This template works in the Northern Hemisphere.

You will need to know two things:
- Are you in the Northern or Southern Hemisphere (see page 6)?
- What **latitude** are you at?

Ask an adult to help you. You can find your latitude by using this NASA link:

mynasadata.larc.nasa.gov/latitudelongitude-finder

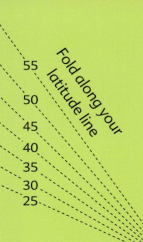

Fold along your latitude line

55 50 45 40 35 30 25

Fold here

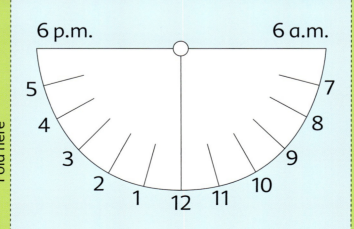

6 p.m.   6 a.m.

5   7
4   8
3   9
2   10
1   12   11

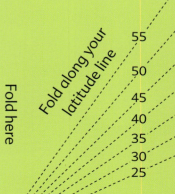

Fold here

Fold along your latitude line

55 50 45 40 35 30 25

2

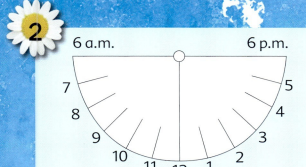

If you live in the Southern Hemisphere, you need to swap the numbers as shown.

3

Cut out your copy of the sundial. Fold the two sides away from the dial face along the fold lines. Carefully fold out the flaps along your location's latitude lines.

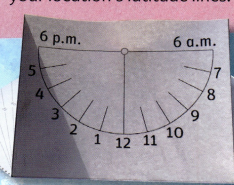

4

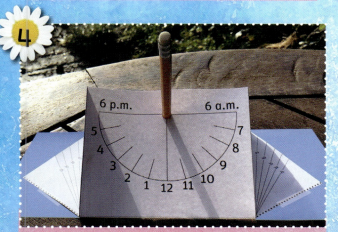

Tape your sundial onto a sheet of card stock. Ask an adult to push the pencil through the circle as shown, at right angles to the face of the dial. Tape it in place onto the card stock.

WHAT'S HAPPENING?

If you turn the sundial so the pencil points due north (or due south if you are in the Southern Hemisphere) the shadow from the pencil will point to the time. The sundial still works in winter. The Sun will shine up from below the dial's face, with the shadow visible through the thin paper. Remember to subtract an hour if you are on daylight saving time.

What Is an Equinox?

Have you noticed that the Sun is in a slightly different place at the same time each day? It only appears at exactly the same location twice, in March during the spring **equinox**, and September during the fall equinox. An equinox is when the Sun is over the Earth's equator, and the hours of daylight and darkness are about equal. The only place on the Earth where the Sun's location matches every day is on the equator itself.

YOU WILL NEED:

- 2 foot by 2 foot (60 cm x 60 cm) wooden or cardboard square
- long pencil
- another pencil
- large lump of modeling clay
- some chalk

1

Push the long pencil into a ball of modeling clay. Place it on a corner of the board. Firmly press the clay to the board and tape it in place.

2

Place your board on a flat surface in sunlight. Note the time of day. Place a dot at the tip of shadow on the board using the other pencil. Write the date.

3

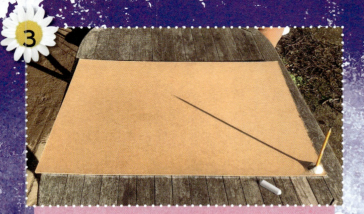

The board must be in exactly the same place each time you take a reading. Mark its position using chalk, or find a place you can leave the board for the whole experiment.

4

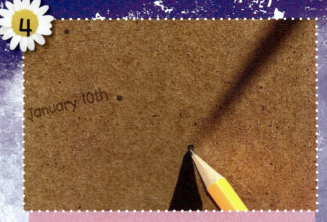

January 10th

Take a reading every day or every week at exactly the same time. You will see that the shadow moves by a tiny amount each day.

WHAT'S HAPPENING?

Your shadow readings change location because Earth faces the Sun at an angle. As Earth orbits around the Sun, its position is changing all the time, and so are the length of the days. If you did this experiment for a whole year and joined the dots, your readings would look like this:

June   December

Meteoroid Crater

A **meteoroid** is a particle or rock traveling through space. Sometimes they hit Earth. Large meteoroids leave craters when they hit, and toss up rock and dirt, known as **ejecta**. Try this experiment to see how the size, angle, and speed of a meteoroid affects the size and shape of the craters and the ejecta.

YOU WILL NEED:

- shallow tray or cat litter box
- bag of unbleached flour
- instant cocoa
- pebbles
- ruler
- pen and notepad

1

Fill the tray with flour until it is around 1 1/2 inches (4 cm) deep. Sprinkle a layer of cocoa on the surface.

2

Take a small pebble and drop it from eye level into the tray. Measure the crater (dent) and draw the shape of the ejecta (the flour).

3

Now drop a medium size pebble from the same height. Measure the crater and the shape of the ejecta and record your result.

4

Smooth the flour and sprinkle on more cocoa after each drop. Try dropping similar size pebbles from different heights and record the results.

Once you have lots of records to match to, choose a pebble and ask a friend to drop it into the tray without you seeing. Can you figure out what height they dropped it from?

WHAT'S HAPPENING?

These space rocks travel so fast they hit the ground with a huge force. That force usually moves a lot more dirt than just the size of the meteoroid itself. The rock that made the vast Meteor Crater in Arizona was probably only about 164 feet (50 meters) in diameter!

Marshmallow Stars

Ancient people thought some constellations looked like the outlines of legendary people, or creatures. The constellations pictured below are linked with birth signs. Try creating your birth sign constellation using toothpicks and marshmallows. Then—you can eat it!

YOU WILL NEED:
- dark paper
- chalk
- marshmallows
- toothpicks
- scissors

1

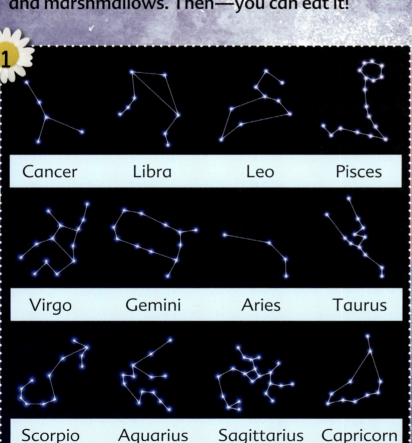

| Cancer | Libra | Leo | Pisces |

| Virgo | Gemini | Aries | Taurus |

| Scorpio | Aquarius | Sagittarius | Capricorn |

Find a picture of your favorite constellation. We chose Libra. See if you can find your constellation in the night sky. Libra is quite hard to see, as none of the stars are very bright.

The study of birth signs is called **astrology**. It has nothing to do with the science of astronomy. Astrologers believe the position of stars and planets influence our lives.

2

Find scissors strong enough to cut toothpicks.

3

Draw a plan of how the marshmallows will connect together to make your constellation.

4

Make your constellation using toothpicks and marshmallows. Cut the toothpicks to get the distances between stars correct.

WHAT'S HAPPENING?

As Earth orbits the Sun, the Sun appears to pass in front of different constellations through the year. Oddly, you can't see the particular constellation at night in the month it represents. The Sun is passing through it, so it is not visible in the night sky.

Test Your Astronomy Know-How!

Are you an astronomy genius? Test yourself with these questions. The answers are on page 29.

1. What is astronomy?
a) the study of space   b) cooking in space   c) the study of star signs

2. What should you NEVER look directly at, or it may harm your eyes?
a) the Moon   b) the Sun   c) a rainbow

3. What is a solar eclipse?
a) when the Sun sets at night
b) a tool for looking safely at the Sun
c) when the Moon travels in front of the Sun

4. Which hemisphere are you in if you live above the equator?
a) Northern   b) Southern

5. The Moon creates no light of its own.
a) true   b) false

6. The Sun is vast. How many Earths could fit inside the Sun?
a) 13 b) 1,300,000 c) 130

7. Which planet is Earth's nearest neighbor?
a) Neptune b) Jupiter c) Venus

8. What can an astrolabe help you do?
a) travel to space
b) clean your telescope
c) measure the height of the Sun and Moon

9. Apart from at the equator, how many days a year is the Sun in exactly the same position at the same time of day?
a) 0 b) 2 c) 365

10. What size crater does a meteoroid create when it hits Earth?
a) the crater will be the same size as the meteoroid itself
b) the crater will be smaller than the meteoroid
c) the crater will be larger than the meteoroid

Glossary

asteroids Minor planets between Mars and Jupiter.

astrology The study of the supposed influences of the stars on human affairs.

comets Bright objects in space that develop a cloudy tail.

constellation A group of stars forming a pattern.

ejecta Material that is forced or thrown out after an impact.

equator An imaginary circle around the middle of Earth.

equinox When day and night are of equal length.

galaxies Very large groups of stars and other matter.

gravity A force of attraction between particles or bodies that occurs because of their mass.

hemisphere One of the halves of Earth as divided by the equator.

horizon The line where Earth or the sea seems to meet the sky.

latitude The distance north or south from the equator measured in degrees.

meteoroid A meteor revolving around the Sun.

nebula Huge clouds of gas or dust.

orbit The path taken by one body circling around another body.

phases The shapes of the part of the moon that are visible at different times during a month.

plasma Charged particles.

solar eclipse An eclipse of the Sun by the Moon.

solar system The Sun with the planets, moons, asteroids, and comets that orbit it.

sunspots Dark spots that appear on the Sun's surface.

For More Information

Amson-Bradshaw, Georgia. *Earth and Space*. New York, NY: Gareth Stevens, 2018.

Gardner, Robert. *Science Fair Projects About the Sun and the Moon*. New York, NY: Enslow Publishing, 2017.

Nichols, Michelle. *Astronomy Lab for Kids: 52 Family-Friendly Activities*. Beverly, MA: Quarry Books, 2016.

Prinja, Raman. *Awesome Astronomy: Fantastic Hands-on Activities*. London, UK: QEB Publishing, 2016.

Websites

Due to the changing nature of Internet links, PowerKids Press has developed an online list of websites related to the subject of this book. This site is updated regularly. Please use this link to access the list:

www.powerkidslinks.com/bs/astronomy